THICK OF IT

THE
SEAGULL
LIBRARY OF
GERMAN
LITERATURE

ULRIKE ALMUT SANDIG

THICK OF IT

TRANSLATED BY KAREN LEEDER

Seagull
BOOKS

LONDON NEW YORK CALCUTTA

GOETHE
INSTITUT

This publication was supported by a grant from the Goethe-Institut India

Seagull Books, 2021

Originally published as *Dickicht. Gedichte* by Ulrike Almut Sandig
© Schöffling & Co., Frankfurt 2011

First published in English translation by Seagull Books, 2018
English translation © Karen Leeder, 2018

ISBN 978 0 8574 2 835 6

British Cataloguing-in-Publication Data
A catalogue record for this book is available from the British Library

Typeset and designed by Sunandini Banerjee, Seagull Books
Printed and bound by WordsWorth India, New Delhi, India

CONTENTS

Ulrike Almut Sandig was born in 1979 in rural Großen-hain, in Saxony, part of the former East Germany, as the daughter of a Lutheran pastor and a chemist's assistant. She started life as a kind of guerrilla poet, pasting poems onto lamp posts on the streets of Leipzig with friends and handing them out on flyers and free postcards. These early projects 'augenpost' (eye mail) along with 'ohrenpost' (ear mail) give a sense already of the importance she places on experimenting with genres and approaches, and on freeing poetry from its conventional setting and taking it to the reader, especially a reader who might not have engaged with poetry before. After completing her Masters in Religious Studies and Modern Indology, she graduated from the creative-writing programme of the illustrious German Literary Institute in Leipzig. She has written two volumes of prose texts *Flamingos* (2010) and *Buch gegen das Verschwinden* (Book against Disappearance, 2015);   four volumes of poetry; joined with poet and musician Marlen Pelny on the project 'poetry for friends of pop music' culminating in two CDs; worked on radio plays and audiobooks; and collaborated with several composers and musical, visual and sound artists for various multimedia projects (http://ulrike-almut-sandig.de/).

Since her debut collection *Zunder* (2005), she has won numerous prizes, both for her poetry and her short stories, including the Leonce and Lena prize in 2009, the most important award for young poets in Germany, and the Wilhelm-Lehman-Preis, 2018. In 2017, she was awarded the prestigious 'Text + Language' Literary Prize of the Kulturkreis der deutschen Wirtschaft (Association of Arts and Culture of the German Economy at the Federation of German Industries), and the 'laudatio' highlighted the new perspectives opened by her *oeuvre*, 'the new architectures of sound created in the German language'.

Zunder, an old word meaning tinder, provided a characteristically emphatic arrival. These are poems that burn, crackle and sparkle, shedding light, and darting off in all directions—but also, following a German idiom ('jemandem Zunder geben'), 'giving the readers hell'. Light is a key motif, but so is shadow. Images burn intensely but also burn out while syntax is stretched and grammar distorted. Even its publishing history hints at this intensity: the collection was reissued in a revised format in 2009 with some poems having altered beyond recognition.

Sandig's second collection *Streumen* (2007) picks up the theme of movement which will become so important in the collection presented here. 'Streumen' is at once a (real) place (a tiny, one-street village in Saxony), an activity and a way of being; a neologism made up of an amalgam of German words suggesting strolling, streaming and dreaming. These poems take the reader on a journey through an acoustic landscape that hovers constantly between the real and the imaginary. They play out the tension between the mundane life of home and what Sandig calls a 'sheer longing' that drives the lyric subject to look for unknown vistas—vistas of happiness that might themselves be illusory.

In their own way, both these collections pave the way for the poems presented here, taken from Sandig's 2011 *Dickicht* (meaning thicket or jungle). This collection is about emotional itineraries but, as the title suggests, the poems take us further afield, into a 'thicket' that is at once the world, the psyche and language itself. It is structured into balancing sections entitled 'North' and 'South'. This is a journey, then, through hemispheres and through the imagination, but a journey with a nod to Jules Vernes as it goes through the centre of the earth. At the centre is a single poem that marks that transition, and at the centre of that poem is a line that locates a fissure, a tear 'at the centre of the body'. Thus large historical or geographical concerns constantly inscribe themselves into, and find their way back to, the vital textures of the individual.

The North is a place of cold, of absence, the kampfzone of stunted mountain trees below the snowline, of silence, of dark Nordic myths and austerity. But it is also home, with the allegiances to the daily life that entails—the washing drying too quickly, the tall grass beyond the yard, the dog.

> maybe someone can
> find a use for it all: for your bed
> and my T-shirt, for the flowers
> in the vase, the coffee in the pot
> and the strange shaggy-maned
> mutt that has slipped, [...]
> into the sheets with us

But even as that reality is recalled and recorded with a tender precision, it is under threat, and the poetry is overlaid with a finely tuned longing for a disappearing world. A key theme is loss—old names are forgotten, identities fall away, things disappear from the kitchen, the map, the middle of last week, and everything is on the slide (her most recent prose collection, *Book against Disappearance*, negotiates the shifting layers of rock deep beneath her Saxon home.) And the losses are not simply domestic. When some names disappear, they take communities and larger ways of belonging with them:

> I've been told there is a place
> for all vanished things, like
>
> the old varieties of apple
> clowns and gods and among
>
> them even that good God of Manhattan
> Karl-Marx-Stadt and Constantinople

Increasingly, Sandig thinks of herself as a political poet. Certainly, her 2016 collection *ich bin ein Feld voller Raps verstecke die Rehe und leuchte wie dreizehn Ölgemälde übereinandergelegt* (I am a field full of oil-seed rape give cover to deer and shine like thirteen oil paintings laid one on top of the other), makes this clear with references to forced migration, xenophobia and torture. Yet important themes—memories of the Holocaust, for example, and the way the threat lives on—are present here already even as they are always mapped onto the local, the fractured individual in 'the thick of it' (my version of her title) all.

If the North is a precarious place that threatens to swallow identity, what is the South? That is harder to say. On the one hand, it is a call that echoes through German poetry, from Goethe's 'Mignon's Song' onwards: 'Do you know the land where the lemon orchards blossom?' But it is at once more concrete and more difficult to pin down in her work. Often linked with writing, or fairy tale, or a kind of utopian escape, it is perhaps best thought of as an idea of otherness:

> south is always
> south. south dressed to impress. south
>
> in the wind, at the wide open window. a child.

Rather than understanding North and South as static values, the collection emphasizes again and again the restless and often precarious energy that carries with it its own dangers ('going South', after all): being carried, led or lured away, hunting, disappearing from the world. These are poems which 'practise being away'; insist on movement for its own sake—'en route for nowhere at all'—and it is striking how many figures of flight there are: from the many aeroplanes, birds, gulls, or the geese, memorably bound for the dark side of the moon, to the car journeys, horses and itinerant beasts of one kind or another that flit through the pages.

Yet poetry stands or falls not by its themes or structures but by its language, and this is language at is most crafted and transformative. Blisteringly contemporary, but with a kind of purity too; by turns comic, ironic, sceptical or nostalgic, it is also profoundly musical. The poems explore an urgently urban reality but are splintered with references to nightmares, the Bible, fairy tales, nursery rhymes, hymns, Goethe, Emily Dickinson and Kafka. Sandig abandons the traditional upper-case for sentences and end-of-line punctuation so as to exploit multiple meanings, stretches syntax, plays with idioms (the German 'leicht fallen', for example, 'to fall easy', meaning to come easy to someone), and surfs on patterns of sound: for example, in a pair of poems that set off the formal and intimate second-person address in German, 'Sie' and 'du'. Indeed, poems are often set in pairs, echoing, reflecting, doubling and undermining until little is certain. There are very few titles appearing above the body of the poems. Rather, Sandig uses bold marking for a phrase within the text, thus highlighting its significance but refusing to give it an ultimate interpretive authority. Perhaps we see here one of the shadows of the GDR: the mistrust of hierarchies and the transparency of language.

Critics have sometimes placed her in the august tradition of the modern greats of the German language—Paul Celan or Ingeborg Bachmann—and indeed one of the poems has been selected for an anthology of the best of fifty years of European poetry in translation. But to my mind, she is more slippery, and more playful too. If the poems always seem to be in search of a self, a home, they are also teasingly aware that it is not such an easy thing to catch up with: 'I am a double-voiced bird' as one more recent poem has it, or as Sandig put it in an interview, '[A]t its best a poetry collection becomes the place where you yourself can disappear.' The Jury of the Droste prize in 2012 spoke of her work as 'opening new horizons' and a Munich review described it as 'Steam-Punk that turns and stretches your very soul'. In English she has something of the oblique otherworldliness of Alice Oswald, but also the bite and energy of spoken word cross-over Kate Tempest. And, like Tempest, Sandig is as at home playing in rock venues as she is on the poetry stage. Experiencing these poems (and one does experience them rather than simply read or listen to them—she is a stellar performer), one feels the precariousness I have described, but also a kind of exhilaration (and it was this that lead me to want to translate her, that visceral excitement when know you're in the presence of the real thing). Sandig is one of the most exciting writers of her generation, engaged in a vital alchemy of the here and now. Hers is a voice we urgently need in English and I hope that this collection conveys some of that energy.

Oxford, 2017

The Desire to be an Indian

If only one were an Indian, always alert, leaning into the wind on a racing horse, quivering over the quivering ground, until one let go of the spurs, for there were no spurs, threw away the reins, for there were no reins, and could hardly make out the land ahead as cropped heath, with horse's neck and horse's head already gone.

Franz Kafka

beneath you the earth, always turning. above you
the silhouette of trees against the steep
arc of the sun. the sky is splayed wide open
a moon turning in time. behind you the soundless
peaks of stone covered with ice. before you
the rubble of clouds. far below lies your
home, **you wrote yourself the poem of it**. inside you
the trembling needle that always points
due north, though you've no idea what lies beyond.

NORTH

but I won't say a thing about the way the trees
shimmer in the light, nor about the trees themselves.

not a word about the beech tree in the doctor's yard
while her daughter is dying upstairs, not a word

about the foxglove tree in our own backyard, where
you and I sit out late every night and act like its only

in the poems I write that the doctor's daughter
is real. of the shimmer of the trees in the light

I will give nothing away but the very tips
the tips of the trees that sway in the wind

and the needles that are always green. I will
act like only that flickering, fevered light

stitched into the tips of the fir trees is real.
but not their trunks crowded beneath, never
those **slender shadows**, the forest, the trees themselves.

once I lost a friend to whom I had done wrong. once I lost another whom I'd simply forgotten:

for no reason. once I lost that plastic ring, green as grass, that belonged to my friend and not long after, the friend herself. just why I lost her has slipped my mind too, and also for no reason. not to worry! it stands to reason: **my friends** are in the kampfzone of the forest, where even the trees disappear. they are stooped beneath the wind. one of them wears a plastic ring on her finger, green as grass. I saw it somewhere else once before.

I've been told there is a place
for all vanished things, like

the old varieties of apple
clowns and gods and among

them even that good God of Manhattan
Karl-Marx-Stadt and Constantinople

Benares and Bombay and the names
of too many brown coal villages

fetch up there, I've been told
in the thick of the silver fir wood

that swallows every sound wave
the place is, or **so I've been told**
not marked on any kind of map.

Tamangur

outside the wind is picking up. inside we're still, faces bent over atlases. through the cross of the window panes, the pine trees shoot up over our heads. a forest will soon grow round our room. let's call it 'Tamangur', since all that is there must have a word that can be written down. my brother, my brother, when did we lose our way and find ourselves here, hopelessly lost between the roots of verbs, and did you not mark the way back?

dear sister, my sister, I've forgotten it all: the bread and the birds' names, the time, and the tarmac path home. all those things like streets, like airports, like traffic lights, air travel are marked on other kinds of maps. so let's stay here in our room in the forest that no one, not you, not even I, will ever leave, the second it is spoken (like just now?). outside the pine trees scrape against each other's trunks, the wind reaches into the trees, and I've forgotten their names too. you call them 'the trees with the hard, leathery needles', their nuts, big as fists, drop between the folds of the tree trunks, but do not strike us. you lie in the room. I lie next to you and already don't know who you—

thinking of plants. how I never remember
their names. 'rushes', 'lilies', 'rushes'.

just coming across that same old rustle
of paper in the offices we pass every day

and remembering that. above our heads the cranes
sway in the wind. none of them making a sound.

walking each day. and most days not talking
with anyone else but you. being on guard

against myself and the **foam** on the banks
of the river we circle. foam always loses.

never losing and especially not you.
being here still, the pair of us, most of what

you and I know, in the very next moment
already: forgotten

what the hell. as long as we're walking, watching
my hair fly in the wind, your face in profile.

no. it's not about you, it's about

the seagulls in summer, the gulls
in their flocks, it's about harmless
gulls. it's not about you. though
all the gulls had such tiny faces
just like yours. they flew right
over my house, where you'll never
come back. but no, it's never

about seagulls! it's about the washing
in the garden, hanging in the sun
and drying too quickly. it's about
the weather, it's about all the things
that are still to be said, about things
like sunshine, like winter, like wind
all the birds, and for me it's also
about the dog we had then, that day
in the park, a park without sea
I recall, that barked at the gulls
for so long that in that whole wide sky

there wasn't a single creature to be seen.

no. they never fly south
in the south one is always alone.
I heard them flying by night, at the start
still the flurry of wings, lonely cries
as they soared up high and higher to reach
the moon and land on the darkest side
turned away from the earth, and stand
for a long, long time. wing to wing
huddled close together: geese, **geese**
on the airless, the flying moon.

when the loudspeakers are silent, the spotlights
are dimmed, when the sound of the last **chorus**
has died away behind the scenes of history

when the actors' uniforms have been hung up
and the cleaners have gone home, when the
auditorium stands quiet in the half-light

that's when you get back up on the stage
and say after me: the whole thing was not
real. and no one here came to any harm.

say after me: the whole thing was not STOP

here is the passage from the street back to winter

1938. the small, inconspicuous curtain of history:
a child-size gate in the iron railings, six steps
down to the dried-up riverbed close to the zoo.

waiting two days, having to stand, with their stars, and
being inspected in broad daylight. then finally off
to the station, into the trucks, that's when the first fell

like flies, like chaff. and later again the little wood
of beech + beech + snow. that is where this story ends.
but here is the passage, here's where it all starts aga— STOP

behind my eyes the others sit and watch
everything I see. I only see what I can see.

at night I see the marten in the porchlight
under the foxglove tree, not moving a muscle,

becoming invisible in the fading light. I see
no comets, no satellites. I see nothing but

the scrap of moon and my own reflection
in the glass. by day I see the flash of blurred

green in the garden behind the yard, the pigeon
nodding mechanically, always on the same bush

and high above the jet planes on sorties. I see them, too.
as for the others I see them as little as they see me.

they sit deep inside me.

the light goes out and you're alone once
more. or are you, take care! not alone

after all? did you hear it, pitch-black
the hideous horseman, did you hear

the goblin knotting your hair as you
sleep, did you hear the **nightmare**

bounding from one too-dark corner
across the room to the other, sweeping

its horsey tail over the floorboards?
if it finds you, it will kill itself

laughing or rock you, just touching
your throat—gently till you sleep.

every night the dog forgets to do its duty
and I lie awake, get up, check whether everything's
still there: my neighbour's roof, the hall light, my mutt.
it's almost all here. 'if God will, when the morn doth break'
I will awake and make everything new that has been taken
from me in the night: the skin I have shed, the pain
in my head, this God and the dust, a fresh heart
                                    for the beast.

my dog's heart is too big. my dog is smaller
than usual and shaved clean above his heart.

he lies on the table looking at no one.

in the monitor I see the heart resting in its sac
or rather, not resting: my dog's heart sucks

and pumps and presses against breast bone
and ribs, it beats and sucks and pumps and presses

from inside against the pleura, swollen lining,
the shining inner pelt of all creatures, but

my dog is dry, dry, so dry and still. my dog
makes sounds with his heart and listens to

himself all the while. from outside he sounds
like 'a flying tin can' or 'wound healing over

artificially amplified' or 'things spoken backwards'
or 'purse with a hole'. from inside the dog sounds

different. it hears my murmuring, my 'shsh
shshshshsh', my 'can you still hear me?

'I want to live a few years more.'
the alders have stood for weeks under snow.

inside the gadgets tick. the tube
slips from his mouth as he speaks.

'is it snowing, my child? it's snowing
like that in my lungs, on the x-ray screen,

my wings, I've seen them shine
as they lay there folded and damp

in the jungle of my own breast—
my child, don't you see the Erlking?

the Erlking with crown and train.'
father, I'm hiding my face afraid.

it's snowing again. father is silent
says to himself: 'do you see, my child,

in the winter light the old willow trees
shining so grey. come next year, they'll be

green again.'

always getting up too late and always
too cold. always thinking about going
home, and alone in my room: about me

and nobody else. always wrenching
my own joints when I stretch: you.

not much else. sleeping for weeks as **practice for being away**.
all this in the absence of my own
name. dreaming only twice a month.

once about the bare-branched trees at home.
another time about the fresh snow and how
it buries blankets and pillows and sheets.

just switched the radio on. you look straight ahead.
the engine turns over softly. on the back seat
the child sleeps with eyes wide open. reception
is patchy: from the speakers a roar, no rain
a wall of fog rising before you, a moment ago
it was all still there: your line of sight, the paths cleared
a snowdrift covering the ditches. beside you a slope
falling away, uncertain how deep. **heavy creatures**

in flight—the fog moves over the tarmac like wind
like something soft, just heard, like something blind.

outside the window: light on white metal.
darkness is still far away. tomorrow
far below it will snow, tomorrow

you will have been here forever.
in nine minutes the final descent.
you empty your glass. your thoughts
turn to snow. you pour yourself nothing

of the skies made of ice, that vanish
as if heaven had never existed.

from the plane you see

the smart bluescreens of pools by day
in a thousand and one back gardens

square upon square, as you and I
get closer to Germany. by night

see the blood-orange avenues of lights
of those Persian, Cuban (where are we?)

cities! down below the highways shine
up here it's us that shine. the night arrives

we're making strides—if it's here you have
your child, what will you call it? call it

ASIA, call it ALMUT, call it ALPHA, give
OMEGA a miss. we come from somewhere
we sleep, we're en route for nowhere at all.

was once

a room, that's where you slept. were once
three others, hummed with machines. was once
a body, looked quite like yours. was just a shade
too small and went by your name. wasn't related
was no friend to you, never knew you at all.

day after day the wind blows round the house
rattling the windows. I stand behind them. drift
to and fro, slouching about, sorting out old bits
of paper. I don't go out any more.
if I note something down, I'm repeating myself.
if I note everything down, something comes back:
the pile of paper, the house, my sleeping hours,
all the music I've listened to and everyone else but me.
night after night the wind comes into the house.

I'm lying inside. I hear them swim back
and forth, in pairs, **catfish**: their flat heads,
wide mouths, and whiskers, hardly a sound. you
are one of them, you're not even yourself, you
are heavy and small, you keep wandering
to and fro and (even here!) keep coming after me
calling out to me, I still can't hear what you say
the wind stands, like water, in the way.

it is all done, all
in its place.
all the boxes are
unpacked, the CDs
and books sorted. everything's arrived.
we sit opposite each other
one apple, two cups
of water, to us it tastes like
wine. and all round
are bars of light
dust turning slowly
we don't even notice.

two open windows, wind
blows through the space between us.

forgotten

the weight of our backs. we are leaning
against the tiles, two patches on the slate
two shadow-catchers in the wind-field

in the spotlights of your quarter in autumn.
if you remember, there's nothing more to say.
if I'm too heavy for you, let me up and away.

when I left the afternoon was already over. straggling
children tidied themselves from the playground into the
houses. the first rockets hissed invisibly, still almost inaudible
the throb of the bass. the roadside for quite some distance
was overcast with the haze of **denuded trees,** they smelled

of cuckoo flowers in the woods, and dozing above them the real
clouds in the wind hole, polar light, biting ice. once a chunk
of milk glass fell to the ground in front of me. before I could
tread on it, it melted away. that's when I finally left. after that
I forgot everything here.   I was back by new year.

beyond the last line of streetlamps
there's nothing pointing at the sky, not at
the rockets, the bright colours, that pause

then explode without noise, beyond the last
lights the year ends visibly and absolutely.

beyond that I see nothing. beyond that
my own footsteps crackle in the frost.

I stop in my tracks. at an impossible
distance, the tail lights glow, **friends
still laughing**, out of sight, swerving away.

red rover, red rover

let all my friends come over
let them all come to stay

not go away, let not a single one
leave before the party's done.

let there be no more forest
growing inside us only round us.

let there be wind in the trees
games in the shade, parties like these

until like children in the blue of night
we are taken home, tucked up tight.

I never want to leave here again! don't disappear
like the others. don't head south. there's nothing

greener there than here. hide with me in the
long grass behind the yard. let us stay here and

never go home. but Pat's always mowing the grass.
with him always the colour-blind broker who will

offer him heaven (but it's full of air) in exchange
for the grass. a meadow bird swoops low over

the lawn slicing the broken blue of the sky
from the green. Pat in the thick of it blurring chlorophyll

let's flatten the grass, keep quiet, keep still.

what notes does the earth take from the sky?
all along the highways the blood-orange
lure of dreams, always turning, always the same

carrying news, but what news do they bring?
they point the way for the soundproof sky
in its tightly closed canopy

they point the way to where they will
meet, **to the centre of the world**. and what
does the sky note in response? —quick
as a flash it loses its tail of light.

CENTRE OF THE WORLD

we often kiss each other's faces when they're wet.
we close the horizontal tear running through
the centre of each of our bodies. we sew
ourselves together, we sew ourselves to. let's
make of ourselves, of me and you, one silent creature.

SOUTH

here are the creatures, here the stalls, here you have straw. where there's no one reciting and no one recording, where language is a horse that foams at the mouth, where the reins have been sold off, where your own crazy mare, just like a newborn, stands on the pavement, scraping its hooves and passes through just as our eyelids flicker in concert and someone else is rolling his eyes, where it passes through, alongside the road-markings, and gets smaller towards the edge of the picture, and then disappears, to the place with the lights on, where the others all live. and there you will find those bright ringing horses. there are their stalls and inside the straw. my sleep, my ears, my **hunting song**—be still! there we were perfect. that's where the stalls were and inside the straw.

'write down what we had.' we had
one or two poems, three or four weeks

the city towers as our primeval forest
and we two burrowed deep inside

in the yellow light of a street lamp
between tree trunks of metal and glass.

there was no sun, for the time I was with
you, for that time the rain held at bay.

for that time everything drifted away: all
your money, my shoes, our time and

my dream of creatures in a totally rain-drenched zoo:

a unicorn out for the count, motionless bears
a dripping-wet peacock. high above us a flight

of foxes, we hardly heard them at all.
for, whatever you say, there were two of us
and **everyone else was lost without trace**.

Sydney

every day the north (the equator) edges a little closer.
falcons hang on the wind, half-asleep, looking for
shadow and pigeons, light metal, a stroke of luck.

in the wind gusts the oldest towers creak, the newer ones
tilt at incalculable degrees: like grass, deliberately.

from every flat roof the sound of nests shifting
the squawking, slithering brood. with any luck

the storm will disappear with the sudden nightfall.
wide awake I hold my hand in front of my face. I
will see nothing, say nothing. I will not be here.

record it, my sailor, record what
is still standing, then read it
aloud. maybe someone can find
a use for it all: for your bed
and my T-shirt, for the flowers
in the vase, the coffee in the pot
and the strange shaggy-maned
mutt that has slipped, dripping wet
into the sheets with us. for here it is dry
dry and good. and we three will
lie here as long as we are permitted.
the sky-blue, **the open sea** that
will draw us in, the three of us
(the creature a little ahead of us
perhaps), record it all my sailor:

what the . . . it can come, the open sea,

it can come for us even tomorrow.

it's not known whether the hydraulics failed
or whether it's what they intended, they'd
never spoken, never mailed, they were
strangers. all that's certain for sure is they
failed to get out on the 12th floor, but carried
on up to level 13 where there are no cameras
scanning the scene, where there's not so much
as a security team, the 13th floor that does
not appear on any plan of the building. **what
happened next we do not know**. though the
story goes they glanced at each other, then
glanced over their shoulders, before they each
laid a hand in the other's hand and began to
sway towards the fire escape in a (never-
before-seen) tango. maybe all they wanted to
do was reach the roof and smoke a cigarillo
or two. maybe it was the distant music from
the 14th floor that led them astray—but
about that
we know
nothing

do ghosts remember? which ones do? which
ones don't? and if they do, which organ

might they use? brain, bones, maybe
the eyes, or perhaps, after all, the **ear**?

do they recall the forest of long grass behind
the yard? how the thorns grated as the roses grew

how the pear tree creaked, the magnolia sang
with its turbines of blossom on every twig

brigades of bluebottles inside, how the planes
purred in the insane blue bowl of the sky

—and does someone recall the thrum of the ghosts
in the tops of the trees, in the thicket of air?

under the churchyard the little dead lie, though in fact
they don't lie at all. they kneel or sit, some of them turn
in their graves and some, if there's room, stand upright.

the little dead push up the red earth of the churchyard
with their little skulls, it blisters and bulges, but never
breaks through, just keeps on rising, grumbling quietly.

see how the little dead are rough and impatient! during
the week they give it their all. sunday they take a day off
and listen to the bells: thoughtfully, righteously, tired to death.

first she took him by the hands
then she left him by the ferns

in the furthest part of the forest
alone. time passed in an instant

between the birches the heat flared
then night fell hard one more time

birds slowly swivelled their heads
through 270 degrees to watch him

but he had not marked his way back
to **the glittering cities of central Europe**

with a single crumb of bread.
mushrooms sprouting round his feet

the feel of fur brushing past him
out of nowhere, in front and behind

shadows, above him trees creaked
the southern sky kept on turning

and kept on turning in circles, or
had he just heard that said, or

read it in his friends' books? where
had it gone wrong? had it gone wrong?

and the hail in the morning and the storm at night.
and the rush of air in the attic, the roof tiles from inside,
ill-concealed antennae beneath. the **roar**
on the screen. the gestures of brothers. the circling
of clouds and across the yard creatures flew in a dream

you don't say! and where do you
think you're going with this, after
me, maybe? but can it be, that you
presume no less than dare to use
the intimate address in front of all
these good folk, from this day I
turn my back on you, I'm telling
you, oh yes I do, right to your ugly
kisser, and god help you, mister, if
you go cracking jokes, with that
smirking gob, oh let it be, with that
smirking physog full of poetry,
do you get my drift, you mouthy
clown, or what the hell: you're
going down, your pug-faced gob,
your heart's a dog, have it in
writing, if you presume no less than
dare to use the intimate address,
you go too far, I tell you, this time,
squirt

yours sincerely

just saying: you're a bloke and
older than me, but that don't say
much. just saying: you're stuck in
the doorway to my heart, you
dog, you mule-headed prop, I
can't get you, oh god, out of me,
just strike that from your lousy
heart, outman me when we're
playing rough, start after me,
chase me, yes you, crawl on all
your four paws but, tell me,
mate, since when have we been
intimate? let's just say instead
you are my dog, my pet that is,
hip-hip-hooray, an ugly mug like
yours is quite okay, my sweetest
physog, my heart, I say: give me
a little scratch, I have, I tell you,
given my say so.

behind my eyes
I see you, you are
the man with the two
missing fingers, I am
the girl with the one
missing heart. you stand
eating your dark bread
you stand still, you
look out of the window
outside the pine trees rustle
outside there is no one
waiting for you. I watch you
as you sip your tea
take a look round
for the last time
and go to work on your
portrait of a woman with
close-cropped black
and white hair, not old and
not young, who takes me
aback, in whom you
recognize me, at last.

can you still see me? you won't
recognize me. already we are almost
not there. were you the one who looked right
through me? try again, hard as you can, look closely:
we were
never that pale.
my hand rests on your back which is already lonely
this photo of us, it's developing backwards:
we're losing our focus, we're falling apart,
we're floating on white paper.

this is how it is to sleep in our four arms. your head, my brain, our daily bread can stay outside. and resting so very gently on your temple: my fifth arm. we take it in turns to murmur: **we've shut up shop**. we believe we can fail, we cannot hear what we say, we have four eyes and no longer need them. we squander the nights, we swap while we're sleeping, we switch the scripts, cameras, the rolls of film.

this is how it is with me: one is wide awake and always
turns her back, gets wet the more she dries, always says hi
pulls faces, mutters under her breath and laughs. the other is out
like a light. it's not yet tomorrow. yesterday is today
and today is your and my last day that won't come to an end
should never end. tonight I shall sleep for as long as I can.
I'll sleep and talk with you. I'll sleep and look at you.

since the dog has been gone
I talk a lot. at night the lamps **sway**.
I lie underneath. and during the day
Venice trembles and the rest trembles too:
my chair and my table, my body

my bed. in my sleep I give voice

to the things no longer here. of the dog
enough said. his cushion is empty.
since the dog has been gone
you are no longer with me and I talk
too much. the dog is nowhere to be found.

conversation with the centaur

told me he was descended from
cumulus clouds and didn't mean it

as a metaphor. said he was half-man
half-horse, neither fish nor fowl

not half nor whole and if push came
to shove, he'd prefer to be anyone

else but himself, less filled with rage
and more totally bald, more Ixion

and less wanton or, put another way
more dark horse than bright knight

more stud than man, more beast than
noble steed, he couldn't say, was always

in two minds—at this point exactly
his voice trailed away. we stood

facing each other. I didn't ask
for more. he scraped his hooves.

I stood there a long time staring as
with a sweep of his tail he vanished

into the thicket. his hooves left
deep serifs scored in the ground.

the shoes worn out with dancing

her with her mother's old wedding
dress and a hickey on her neck

him with knots in his scruffy hair
under a scrap-metal crown

and a sadness in his face that would
have been enough to have them both

thrown off the stage for good.
that's how they stood there.

eyes on each other. each holding
each other's gaze, so neither

would move a muscle while the show
went on. that's how long it lasted.

(shoes long ago worn out with dancing)
at some point the curtain fell.

they turned at the same time
turned away.

amongst the arm-length cucumbers, tomatoes
and baby lettuce in the greenhouse lives **John**

the Baptist. he is sullen and full of rage
and some people say he never even

existed. but I got to know him when
I entered the greenhouse one night

looking for herbs for my cooking. the neon
light hummed, humidity rose and there stood

John the Baptist in his skins carefully watering
the pepper and sage. he looked me straight

in the eye and kept shtum about me. but lo
I ran with my heart a wide-open book

and bouquets of sage and a head of lettuce
in my arms, back into the safety of my kitchen.

give me the cut fields under the film of air.

give me the pine trees that tug at the motionless light.

give me the fish pond in the corner, the duckweed on top.

give me the verdigris that darkens so quickly on this house
of mine that stands alone. the clouds roll on past. **open
your eyes!** already the great midday is spreading in every direction.

noon

outside the shadows dwindle
but we are so tired again.

above us the sun stands at midday
around us the thicket of high-rise

buildings: inside couples lie close
and barely know one another.

we are there too, you and me
on the floor. my skin cools against

yours, outside as always the heat
but as always I am too cold. are you

sleeping, my friend? the clock with
one hand dead on top of the other

and someone shouts NO and then again NO
and the shadows between us are growing.

it's certain you can't stay here. certain
too that you'll never get out. you're
stuck here for certain, not one for travel
nor one for being away, though one day
you'll just have to go but that's still so far off
like everything that remains invisible:

those old familiar pains in your head
and the fact they won't disappear,
not at home and not in the south that
remains invisible too, no matter where
you go looking, no odds, south is always
south. **south** dressed to impress. south

in the wind, at the wide open window. a child.

it's certain that **it will all still be there**.
even after sleeping in again, forgetting
you as I slept, then forgetting myself
and the late-film from yesterday night
and all those things that went missing
without trace the day before yesterday
the minute I looked away: knife, fork
and scissors and the light from the fridge
and the salt from the bread, and the plot
and the thread, the smell of my body
and even that nothing was certain, that
of all things was still there.

now that I'm gone, everything comes easy.
wednesday someone selling eggs, thursday
catching fish. friday there's a power cut
later the alarm is set. oh yes. no one says
'sat'day', except me, and I am not there.
one day someone misses me, then buys himself
a treat. **everything comes** easy. each creature
tucked in at night. me apart. but that comes—

you should go when the party's at its peak, you say
and you're still there yourself. I'm still there too.

I say we should be together, with our thighs
mouths, tired tongues and underneath the sinews

the pitiful longing, almost expunged, that is still
there too, we should rub against one another

that's how to chase away sleeplessness, it's
a bottomless box, it's the girl you once saw

with your face to a tee. you are tired and I'm
tired   are you still listening to me?

then let's stay, you and me, let's just stay
sitting right here. until the hunting light falls

as the sun draws near, until the sun stands below
the horizon, the lights go out and until you and I

until we wrap ourselves tight, more tightly, into that
twilight-sleep, in which pain, if there is any pain

will be something felt as if far away
and **the white surface that is your heart** shines

once more and we lie on it as if on a lap without
body, an ancient, almost forgotten song in our ears.

but should you seek me, you will not

find me under the apple-tree cope
where time in the shape of a pig
escaped from the slaughterhouse and
hid itself in the scrub. and not in
the yard, where once in a storm, with
a single tug, a rowan tree lifted its roots
and flew to the fence, and fell back
to earth only then, but that only
in your dream or mine, though it still
counts, whatever you say, for you
won't find me in a dream anyway.
but should you still seek me, and want
to shed light on the question of your
and my time, our runaway time that
will never be found, but should you still
seek me, even then, be at
the right time (meaning: now) at
the right place (meaning: anywhere).
and there you will see what counts.

the mountain of apples stored in the cellar
for generations, the heart of the building
above and the yard and the garden and
a certain way off the frantic haircuts
of the credit in its safe in all the banks we know
in fact **all that you and I know** does not count.

but should you find me, all that does not count
will be left behind.
                              then I will make anew
all that we, me and you, do not recognize
straight away, but recall quite clearly, nonetheless.

I've made this **song**
using only words.
it sounds like the clack
of the pedestrian light
on red, but also like
the clatter of conkers
on impact, like
the motionless crows
on the lawn by the train
the swaying of cranes
over the grass, like
the unexplained shutdown
of all trains into town, like
the pacemaker of the woman
sitting next to you, tick tick-tock
tick-tock tick tick-tock
STOP but does my song also
sound like that good old
'lay thee down now and rest,
may thy slumber be,' do you
hear my song? let my song
never come to an end! my
song won't ever end, as long
as I myself don't end.

but now here's a song
I made without using

words at all. hold
tight! this is where
it all starts for real:

∞

when the last song is done, when
the sine wave of the last chord

is moving off towards the horizon ∞
in small and smaller and almost

imperceptible waves, when the vinyl disc
has stopped turning, the diamond stylus

circles, when from the two blue speakers
an ocean almost vanished softly roars

when the heart chambers flicker, and when
you are with me and hear all of this

then go and tell the others too: we
have **taken leave** of our senses

but can still, still, just be heard.

Notes

'The Desire to be a Indian', from Franz Kafka's *Betrachtung* (*Meditation*), 1913.

PAGE 10 | **Tamangur**

The 'God da Tamangur' is an alpine forest of stone pines at about 2,300 metres altitude in Switzerland, a few kilometres south along the S-charl valley in the community of Scuol in Unterengadin. In a poem of 1923, the Engadine poet Peider Lansel made the Tamangur the symbol of his native language, Romansch. If you visit the forest in winter, you need snow shoes and to know that on entering the forest your own voice might go missing too.

PAGE 15 | **being inspected**

On 10 November 1938, in Leipzig, several hundred Jews were gathered up in the walled-in riverbed of the Parthe and displayed to the townsfolk. From there, 550 Jewish men were taken to the railway station and loaded onto trains destined for Buchenwald and Sachsenhausen. The memorial stone on the banks of the river Parthe is made of green diabase, 'diabasis', being Greek for 'passage, transit'.

PAGE 18 | **for the beast**

'morgen früh, wenn Gott will' is a line from the lullaby 'Guten Abend, gute Nacht' (Good evening, good night) included by Arnim and Brentano in their celebrated collection of German folksongs *Des Knaben Wunderhorn* and well known through Brahms' Lullaby setting, op. 49 no. 4. There is another echo in the song before last in this volume. The best-known English version, 'Lay thee down now and rest, / May thy slumber be blessed', does not have the same anxiety about waking as the German, hence this alternative version.

PAGE 24 | from the plane
This quotes the famous German children's song for St Martin's day (11th November): 'Ich geh mit meiner Laterne' (I go with my lantern).

PAGE 32 | let's flatten the grass, keep quiet, keep still
In a letter to a friend, Emily Dickinson writes: 'If roses had not faded, and frosts had never come and one had not fallen here and there whom I could not awaken, there were no need of other Heaven than the one below, and if God had been here this summer, and seen the things that *I* have seen—I guess he would think His Paradise superfluous' (*Letters*, 329). After she was thirty, the American poet never left her house and garden again. Patrick Ward, who helped in and about the house for many years (and from whom in my poem the old colour-blind broker wants to buy this paradise), was called Pat by Dickinson. Ward was later one of the coffin-bearers at Dickinson's funeral.

PAGE 69 | song
This song without music is a response to 'Three Songs without Words', a concerto for clarinet and piano, by the Israeli composer Paul Ben Haim.

BOUQUETS

The poet would like to thank The German Literature Institute, Leipzig, the Goethe Institute, Sydney; the Künstlerhaus Edenkoben, the Literarisches Colloquium Berlin, and the Cultural Foundation of the Canton Thurgau for time, Sebastian Reuter for appearing unexpectedly at the end of the book and Marlen Pelny for reading and rereading.

Translator's Acknowledgements

Some of these poems, or versions of them, have appeared in *Asymptote*, *Cordite Poetry Review*, *MPT*, *New Books in German*, the chapbook *PEN America* (2016), and *SPORT*. A further selection was featured in the BBC 4 radio programme 'Mother Tongue' curated by Helen Mort, in July 2017. 'Being inspected' was included in the *MPT* volume *Centres of Cataclysm*: *Fifty Years of MPT*, edited by Sasha Dugdale and David and Helen Constantine (Bloodaxe Books, 2016). A selection of these translations won an award from the Literarisches Colloquium, Berlin (2014); the English PEN EUNIC New Voices, European Literature in Translation Pitch (2016) and an American PEN PEN/Heim Translation Fund award (2016).

I would like to thank Fergus Barrowman and Sally-Ann Spencer of *SPORT* for the original invitation, English PEN, the American PEN/Heim Translation Fund, Poet in the City, *MPT*, the Vice Versa workshop at the LCB, and the Knowledge Exchange Fellowship of TORCH (Oxford University) for making work on this project possible. And Ulrike Almut Sandig and her family for making it a joy.